Pebble® Plus

First Ladies
Eleanor Roosevelt

by Sally Lee

Consulting Editor: Gail Saunders-Smith, PhD

Consultant: Carl Sferrazza Anthony, Historian
National First Ladies' Library
Canton, Ohio

CAPSTONE PRESS
a capstone imprint

Pebble Plus is published by Capstone Press,
1710 Roe Crest Drive, North Mankato, Minnesota 56003.
www.capstonepub.com

Library of Congress Cataloging-in-Publication Data
Lee, Sally.
Eleanor Roosevelt / by Sally Lee.
p. cm—(Pebble plus. First Ladies)
Summary: "Simple text and photographs describe the life of Eleanor Roosevelt"—Provided by publisher.
Includes bibliographical references and index.
ISBN 978-1-4296-5010-6 (library binding)
ISBN 978-1-4296-5603-0 (paperback)
1. Roosevelt, Eleanor, 1884–1962—Juvenile literature. 2. Presidents' spouses—United States—Biography—Juvenile
literature. I. Title. II. Series.
E807.1.R48L44 2011
973.917092—dc22   2009053406

Editorial Credits
Christine Peterson, editor; Ashlee Suker, designer; Svetlana Zhurkin, media researcher; Eric Manske,
        production specialist

Photo Credits
Corbis, 9; Bettmann, 12–13
Franklin D. Roosevelt Library, 5, 6–7, 21
Getty Images/Keystone, 1, 15, 18–19; Keystone/Bachrach, 11; Time & Life Pictures/David E. Scherman, 17; Time Life
        Pictures/Leo Rosenthal, cover (right)
Shutterstock/Alaettin Yildirim, 5, 7, 9, 11, 13, 17, 19 (caption plate); antoninaart, cover (left), 1, 4–5, 10–11, 22–23, 24
        (pattern); Gemenacom, 5, 11 (frame)

Note to Parents and Teachers

The First Ladies series supports national history standards related to people and culture. This
book describes and illustrates the life of Eleanor Roosevelt. The images support early readers
in understanding the text. The repetition of words and phrases helps early readers learn new
words. This book also introduces early readers to subject-specific vocabulary words, which are
defined in the Glossary section. Early readers may need assistance to read some words and to
use the Table of Contents, Glossary, Read More, Internet Sites, and Index sections of the book.

Printed in the United States of America in North Mankato, Minnesota.
012012
006536CGVMI

Table of Contents

Early Years

Eleanor Roosevelt sparkled
as first lady. But as a child,
she was shy. Eleanor was born
October 11, 1884.
Her parents, Elliott and Anna,
were among the richest people
in New York City.

born in New
York City

1884

young Eleanor in 1887

Eleanor's father made her
feel special. Her pretty mother
made Eleanor feel plain.
Eleanor's parents died
when she was young.
At age 8, Eleanor went to live
with her strict grandmother.

born in New
York City

1884

In 1891, Eleanor's family included her father, Elliott (left), and brothers Elliott Jr. (right) and Gracie Hall (seated).

7

Growing Up

In 1899 Eleanor went

to the Allenswood Academy

in England. She was shy.

Her teacher thought

Eleanor was smart.

She helped Eleanor

become more confident.

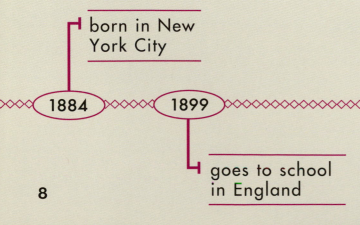

born in New
York City

1884   1899

goes to school
in England

Eleanor (back row, center) with classmates at Allenswood Academy in 1900

In 1905 Eleanor married her

distant cousin Franklin Roosevelt.

They had six children.

Eleanor liked to help others.

She taught women

about politics. She volunteered

with the Red Cross.

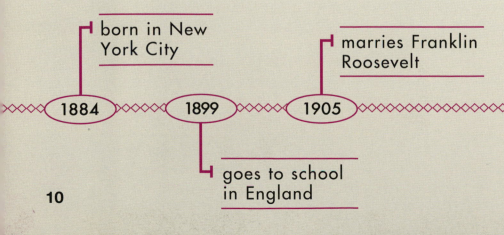

born in New
York City

marries Franklin
Roosevelt

1884   1899   1905

goes to school
in England

Eleanor and Franklin with five of their six children in 1915

First Lady

In 1933 Franklin became
U.S. president. At that time,
millions of Americans needed
jobs, homes, and food.
Eleanor visited poor people.
She told the president
about their problems.

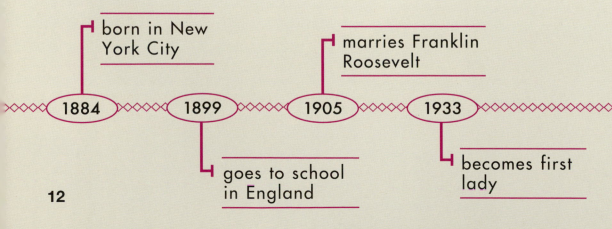

born in New
York City

marries Franklin
Roosevelt

1884 — 1899 — 1905 — 1933

goes to school
in England

becomes first
lady

In 1935 Eleanor visited coal workers.

Eleanor was an

active first lady.

She wrote a column

in the newspaper.

She fought for civil rights.

Eleanor spoke out against

poor working conditions.

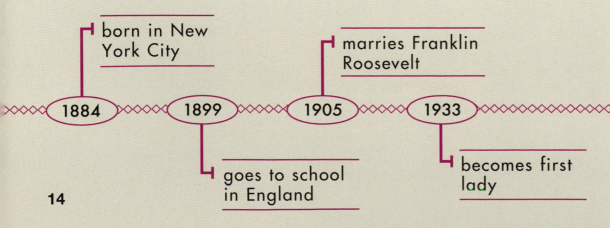

born in New
York City

marries Franklin
Roosevelt

1884   1899   1905   1933

goes to school
in England

becomes first
lady

In 1941 the United States

entered World War II.

Eleanor met with U.S. troops

around the world.

She visited soldiers

in hospitals and wrote letters

to their families.

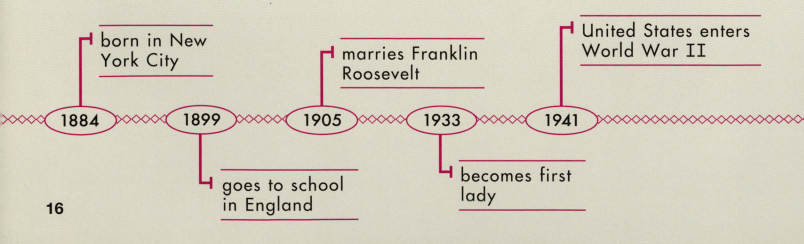

born in New
York City

marries Franklin
Roosevelt

United States enters
World War II

1884   1899   1905   1933   1941

goes to school
in England

becomes first
lady

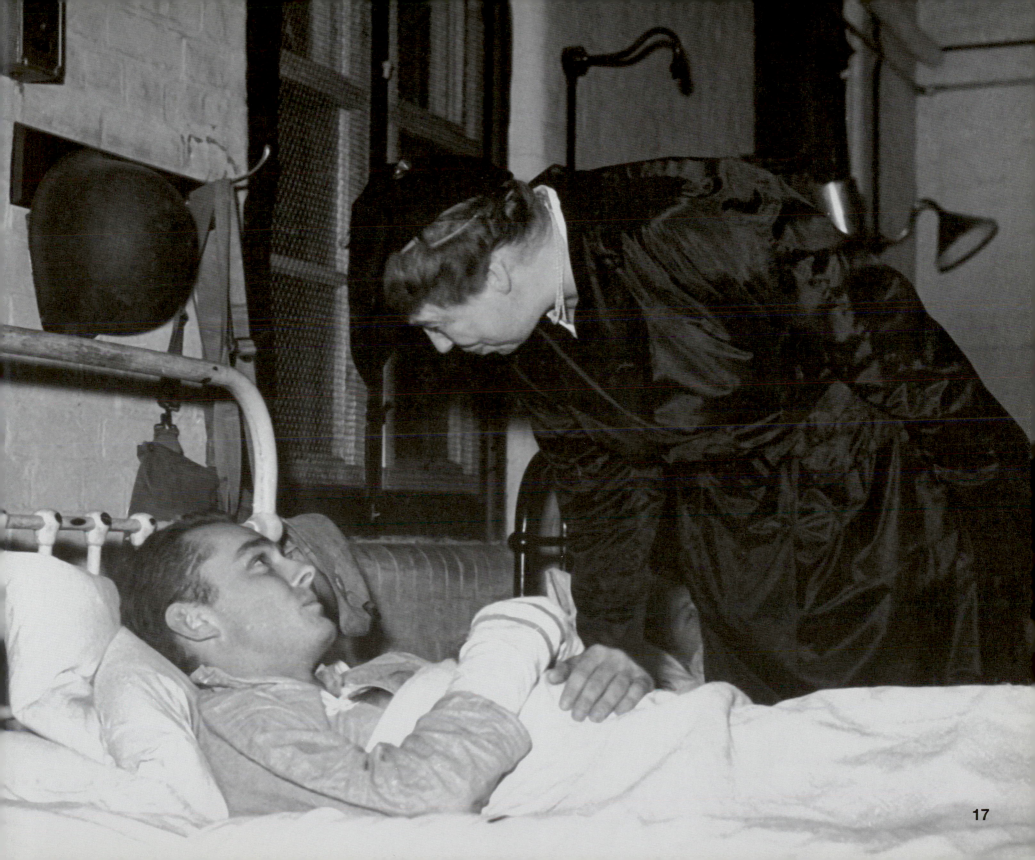

On Her Own

Franklin died in 1945.

Eleanor missed him

but kept working. She worked

for the United Nations.

She helped write a paper

on human rights. She believed

everyone has the same rights.

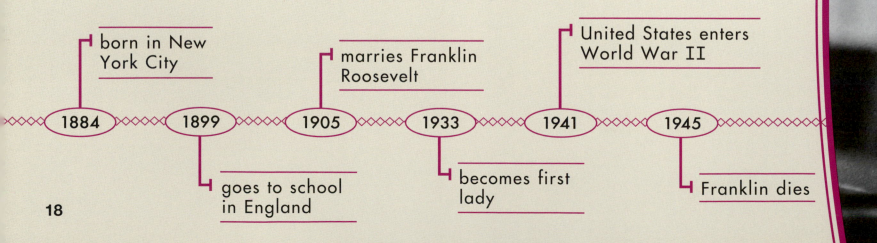

born in New
York City

1884

goes to school
in England

1899

marries Franklin
Roosevelt

1905

becomes first
lady

1933

United States enters
World War II

1941

Franklin dies

1945

Eleanor worked for the United Nations for seven years.

19

Eleanor died in 1962

at age 78.

She is remembered for

working hard to make life

better for all people.

Many people called her

the First Lady of the World.

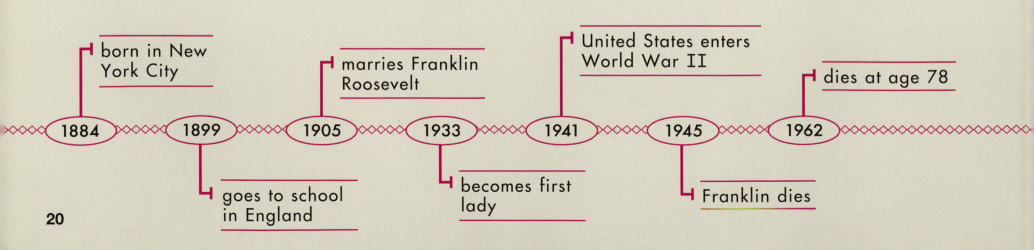

born in New
York City

marries Franklin
Roosevelt

United States enters
World War II

dies at age 78

1884   1899   1905   1933   1941   1945   1962

goes to school
in England

becomes first
lady

Franklin dies

Glossary

civil rights—the rights that all people have to freedom and equal treatment under the law

column—a piece of writing by the same person, or on the same subject, that appears regularly in a newspaper or a magazine

confident—having a strong belief in your own abilities

politics—the act or science of governing a city, state, or country

Red Cross—an organization that gives food, clothing, and money to people after floods, earthquakes, war, and other terrible events

strict—making someone follow rules and behave in a proper way

United Nations—a group of countries around the world that works for peace

volunteer—to offer to do something without pay

Read more

Collard, Sneed B. *Eleanor Roosevelt: Making the World a Better Place*. American Heroes. New York: Marshall Cavendish Benchmark, 2009.

Ford, Carin T. *Franklin D. Roosevelt: The 32nd President*. Heroes of American History. Berkeley Heights, N.J.: Enslow Elementary, 2006.

Internet Sites

FactHound offers a safe, fun way to find Internet sites related to this book. All of the sites on FactHound have been researched by our staff.

Here's all you do:

Visit *www.facthound.com*

FactHound will fetch the best sites for you!

Index

Word Count: 260
Grade: 1
Early-Intervention Level: 22